PRAISE FOR
GRATITUDE WITH ATTITUDE

"When I was asked to write a testimonial for this book, I was thrilled. Why? Because I believe that, along with forgiveness, being grateful is one of the most important things we can do to increase our happiness. That is why you need to buy this book. It will help bring more joy into your life by encouraging you to be more appreciative and thankful for everything in it. And it will do so in a very fun way."

—Allen Klein
Author of *Positive Thoughts for Troubling Times*

"What's so great about this book? *Everything!* Listen, we all know we should be keeping lists of what we're grateful for. But frankly, it feels dull day after day just listing things—even when they are happy-inducing things. Ronnie has solved that by giving us a journal that is vibrant and teeming with creativity and joy. *Gratitude with Attitude* is like a party between the pages. It's fun to be mindful! It's playful to appreciate! Filling out the pages of this journal each evening inspires me to think a little differently about who I am and how I live my days. It invites me to respond with more imagination and zest. At the end of the day, I'm oh-so-grateful for this book!"

—Sherry Richert Belul
Author of *Say It Now* and founder of Simply Celebrate

"The science is in—being grateful and writing about it boosts mental, physical, and emotional health. But are you doing it? Put this 'fill in the blanks journal' by your bedside, and watch your life trajectory shift toward the positive. The pages compel the reader to put pen to paper and respond to whimsical prompts and captivating questions. Daily practice takes consistency and surprise to stay fresh, *Gratitude with Attitude* has that mix. I can't wait to see where it takes me."

—Elise Marie Collins
Author of *Super Ager: You Can Look Younger, Have More Energy, a Better Memory, and Live a Long and Healthy Life*

"'If the only prayer you ever say in your entire life is *thank you*, it will be enough,' wrote Meister Eckhart, the thirteenth century German mystic, theologian, and philosopher. His words are not only wise, they're practical—just like this book. Gratitude is not just a feeling—expressing gratitude is a tool for abundance, and it's a practical path to a happier life. This marvelous new book will show you the way. Read it and reap... great results!"

—B. J. Gallagher
Coauthor of *Your Life Is Your Prayer*

GRATITUDE
with
ATTITUDE

GRATITUDE
with
ATTITUDE

HOW JOURNALING THANKFULNESS
FOR JUST 5 MINUTES A DAY
CAN CHANGE YOUR LIFE

RONNIE WALTER

mango
PUBLISHING

Mango Publishing
CORAL GABLES

For permission requests, please contact the publisher at:
Mango Publishing Group
2850 S Douglas Road, 2nd Floor
Coral Gables, FL 33134 USA
info@mango.bz

For special orders, quantity sales, course adoptions and corporate sales, please email the publisher at sales@mango.bz. For trade and wholesale sales, please contact Ingram Publisher Services at customer.service@ingramcontent.com or +1.800.509.4887.

Gratitude with Attitude: How Journaling Thankfulness for Just 5 Minutes a Day Can Change Your Life

Library of Congress Cataloging-in-Publication number: 2019944256
ISBN: (print) 978-1-64250-128-5, (ebook) 978-1-64250-129-2
BISAC category code SELF-HELP / Journaling

Printed in the United States of America

To Jim,
with love and gratitude always.

Foreword

I first met Ronnie twenty years ago on a sunny Saturday in a community education class in downtown Minneapolis. We sat side by side. I was a newish author, hugely pregnant and extremely uncomfortable; she was a seasoned illustrator and the funniest person I had ever met. We were both in class to learn "how to be ubiquitous." In other words, how did we, as writers and creators, show up in enough places seemingly all at once so the average consumer concludes, "Wow, I *need* to know this person and what she's about."

Fast forward to today. Ronnie and I are still friends living many miles apart. I'm no longer pregnant, she's still warm and funny, and I'm truly honored to add fresh encouragement to Ronnie's long-standing passion for touching lives and hearts through this new gem of a book, *Gratitude with Attitude: How Journaling Thankfulness for Just 5 Minutes a Day Can Change Your Life.*

The power of gratitude is indeed a ubiquitous and proven message; giving thanks for what we have improves our mental well-being. Focusing on what we have moves us from lack to abundance. "Great, but I don't need *another* to-do," you might think. I get it. I have trouble remembering to take my one multi-vitamin. Ronnie gets it too, which is why her journal is exactly the way it is: practical, useful, inviting, and warm—a reflection of the artist herself.

Some twenty years ago, Ronnie and I agreed we may never achieve true personal ubiquity (there are a lot of YouTubers vying for those spots), but if I can let one more person know about the beautiful soul behind this quest to cultivate happier hearts, I can add that to the top of *my* gratitude list.

Gratefully yours,
Marianne Richmond
Bestselling author and illustrator

INTRODUCTION

Hello, I am so grateful you are here!

I've never been a very good journal-keeper. Most of the gratitude journals I've seen felt sooo serious, and they often left me bored with the format. And, even though I have much to be grateful for each day, I would lose interest in them. They were just not me, and, if you're reading this, perhaps they aren't working for you either. After all, everybody looks at the world a little sideways on occasion and feels the need to color outside the lines!

But—I do believe in taking a moment each day to reflect on what we are grateful for, a moment to celebrate even the small things in our journeys. Big "A-Ha" victories don't happen that often, but every day CAN bring us a little more clarity and a little more insight. A journal helps capture those magical little moments: all those sparkly jewels in your life.

So, let's talk about *Gratitude with Attitude.* Each day's section includes:

- An area to write up to three things you are grateful for.

- A place for a tidbit that was a bit "extra" (something that made you smile, think, you found interesting, etc.).

- A place to celebrate a small victory you experienced that day. Hey, it might be as simple as the fact you *actually ate a salad* or stopped yourself from rolling your eyes at someone!

- And, to start things off in the right direction the next day, there's a place to write down an intention you'd like to carry with you to the next morning. You might consider using words like:

peace joy fun open optimistic clarity abundance calm courage balance wonder purpose empathy patience opportunity serenity

And here's the cool part: filling out your daily entry only takes five minutes! Just five minutes—even *I* have the patience for that!

I hope this journal is one you reach for every day when you take a moment to be grateful for the small kindnesses, laughs shared, and all the love surrounding you. And, again, I am so grateful that you are using this little book to record them!

Ronnie

DATE:

So Grateful
Today For:

WELL, THIS WAS
interesting!

Today's Tiny Victory:

Tomorrow's Intention:

DATE:

So Grateful
Today For:

① ② ③

Well, This Was Pretty
AWESOME:

Today's Tiny Victory:

Tomorrow's Intention:

Date:

This made me smile:

Today's Tiny Victory...

VERY **VERY** GRATEFUL FOR:

1.)

2.)

3.)

Tomorrow's Intention:

Today's Tiny Victory:

DATE:

THIS WAS PRETTY COOL:

WOW!

I AM SUPER GRATEFUL FOR:

1

2

3

TOMORROW'S INTENTION

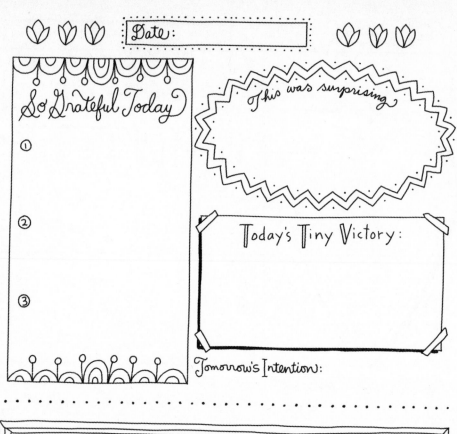

Date:

So Grateful Today

①

②

③

This was surprising

Today's Tiny Victory:

Tomorrow's Intention:

my DREAMS

date:

Today I am Grateful for:

① ② ③ + one more!

Well, this was pretty cool:

TODAY'S TINY VICTORY

TOMORROW'S INTENTION:

SO VERY GRATEFUL FOR...

① ② ③

This made me smile

DATE:

TODAY'S TINY VICTORY

Tomorrow's Intention:

DATE:

So very Grateful

1.

2.

3.

Today's Tiny Victory:

That Was Interesting!

tomorrow's intention:

- - - - - - - - - - - -

Date:

Today I Am Grateful For:

1

2

3

TODAY'S tiny VICTORY

OKAY... THIS WAS INTERESTING!

Tomorrow's Intention:

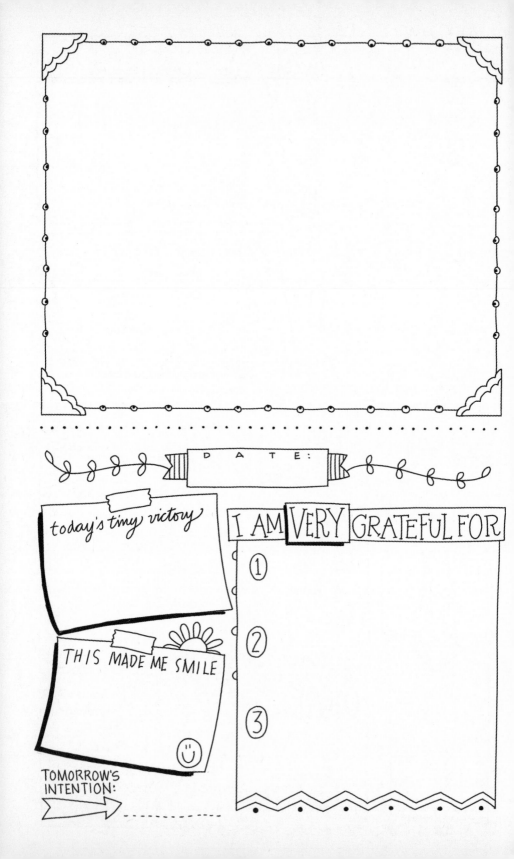

DATE:

today's tiny victory

THIS MADE ME SMILE

I AM VERY GRATEFUL FOR

①

②

③

TOMORROW'S
INTENTION:

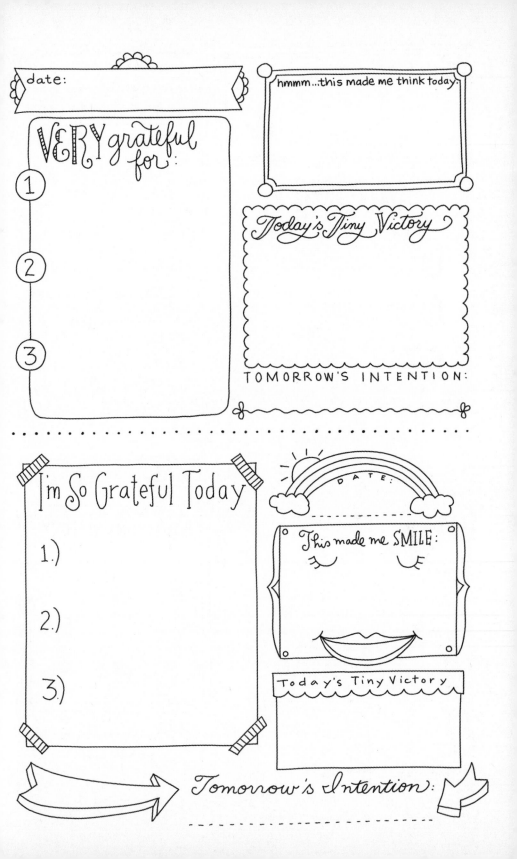

date:

hmmm...this made me think today:

VERY grateful for:

1

2

3

Today's Tiny Victory

TOMORROW'S INTENTION:

I'm So Grateful Today

1.)

2.)

3.)

DATE:

This made me SMILE:

Today's Tiny Victory

Tomorrow's Intention:

Today's Tiny Victory:

DATE:

THIS WAS PRETTY COOL:

WOW!

I AM SUPER GRATEFUL FOR:

1

2

3

TOMORROW'S INTENTION

SO VERY GRATEFUL FOR...

① ② ③

DATE:

TODAY'S TINY VICTORY

This made me smile

❀ Tomorrow's ❀ Intention:

DATE:

So Grateful Today For: ⇨ ⇨ ⇨

WELL, THIS WAS interesting!

Today's Tiny Victory:

TOMORROW'S INTENTION:

DATE:

So Grateful Today For:

①

②

③

Well, This Was Pretty AWESOME:

Today's Tiny Victory!

TOMORROW'S INTENTION:

DATE:

Today, I Am Grateful For:

1

2

3

TODAY'S tiny VICTORY

OKAY... THIS WAS INTERESTING!

Tomorrow's Intention:

What If I...?*

* consider the possibilities!

Date:

So Grateful Today

①
②
③

This was surprising

Today's Tiny Victory:

Tomorrow's Intention:

DATE:

today's tiny victory

THIS MADE ME SMILE

TOMORROW'S INTENTION:

I AM VERY GRATEFUL FOR

①
②
③

DATE:

So very Grateful

1.

2.

3.

Today's Tiny Victory:

That Was Interesting!

tomorrow's intention:

- - - - - - - - - - - - - - -

Today's Tiny Victory:

DATE:

THIS WAS PRETTY COOL:

WOW!
I AM SUPER GRATEFUL FOR:

1

2

3

TOMORROW'S INTENTION

Date:

This made me smile:

Today's Tiny Victory...

VERY **VERY** GRATEFUL FOR:

1.)

2.)

3.)

Tomorrow's Intention:

date:

Today I am Grateful for:

① ② ③ + one more!

Well, this was pretty cool:

TODAY'S TINY VICTORY

TOMORROW'S INTENTION:

SO VERY GRATEFUL FOR...

① ② ③

DATE:

TODAY'S TINY VICTORY

This made me smile

❀ Tomorrow's ❀ Intention:

Date:

So Grateful Today

①

②

③

This was surprising

Today's Tiny Victory:

Tomorrow's Intention:

Lately I've been thinking...

I'm So Grateful Today

1.)

2.)

3.)

DATE:

This made me SMILE:

Today's Tiny Victory

Tomorrow's Intention:

- -

DATE:

So Grateful Today For:

WELL, THIS WAS interesting!

Today's Tiny Victory:

Tomorrow's Intention:

DATE:

So Grateful Today For:

①

②

③

Well, This Was Pretty AWESOME:

Today's Tiny Victory:

TOMORROW'S INTENTION:

date:

VERY grateful for:

①

②

③

hmmm...this made me think today:

Today's Tiny Victory

TOMORROW'S INTENTION:

Today's Tiny Victory:

DATE:

THIS WAS PRETTY COOL:

WOW!

I AM SUPER GRATEFUL FOR:

1

2

3

TOMORROW'S INTENTION

DATE:

So very Grateful

1.

2.

3.

Today's Tiny Victory:

That Was Interesting!

tomorrow's intention:

Date:

This made me smile:

Today's Tiny Victory...

VERY **VERY** GRATEFUL FOR:

1.)

2.)

3.)

Tomorrow's Intention:

Date:

So Grateful Today

①

②

③

This was surprising

Today's Tiny Victory:

Tomorrow's Intention:

SO VERY GRATEFUL FOR..

①

②

③

This made me smile

DATE:

TODAY'S TINY VICTORY

Tomorrow's Intention:

date:

VERY grateful for:

1

2

3

hmmm...this made me think today:

Today's Tiny Victory

TOMORROW'S INTENTION:

I'm So Grateful Today

1.)

2.)

3.)

DATE:

This made me SMILE:

Today's Tiny Victory

Tomorrow's Intention:

I'm So Grateful Today

1.)

2.)

3.)

DATE:

This made me SMILE:

Today's Tiny Victory

Tomorrow's Intention:

Today's Tiny Victory:

WOW!

I AM SUPER GRATEFUL FOR:

1

2

3

DATE:

THIS WAS PRETTY COOL:

TOMORROW'S INTENTION

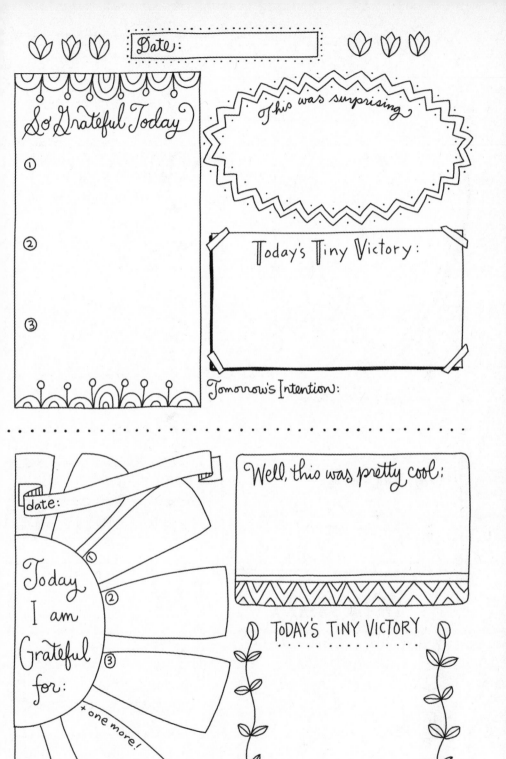

Date:

So Grateful Today
①
②
③

This was surprising

Today's Tiny Victory:

Tomorrow's Intention:

date:

Today I am Grateful for:
①
②
③
+ one more!

Well, this was pretty cool:

TODAY'S TINY VICTORY

TOMORROW'S INTENTION:

Date:

This made me smile:

Today's Tiny Victory...

VERY **VERY** GRATEFUL FOR:

1.)

2.)

3.)

Tomorrow's Intention:

Today's Tiny Victory:

DATE:

THIS WAS PRETTY COOL:

WOW!

I AM SUPER GRATEFUL FOR:

1

2

3

TOMORROW'S INTENTION

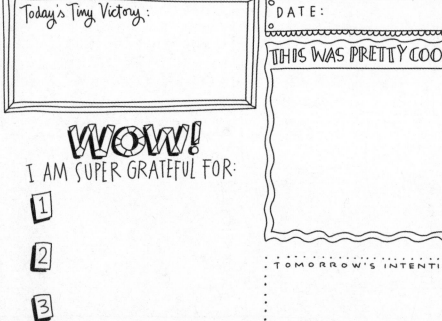

Date:

So Grateful Today

①

②

③

This was surprising

Today's Tiny Victory:

Tomorrow's Intention:

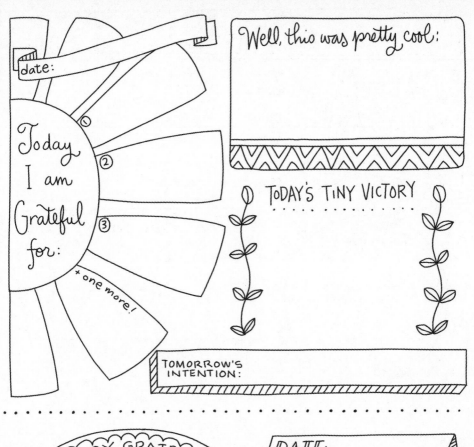

date:

Today I am Grateful for:

① ② ③

+ one more!

Well, this was pretty cool:

TODAY'S TINY VICTORY

TOMORROW'S INTENTION:

SO VERY GRATEFUL FOR:

① ② ③

This made me smile

DATE:

TODAY'S TINY VICTORY

Tomorrow's Intention:

DATE:

So very Grateful

1.

2.

3.

Today's Tiny Victory:

That Was Interesting!

tomorrow's intention:

- - - - - - - - - - - - - - - - - - -

Date:

Today, I Am Grateful For:

1

2

3

TODAY'S tiny VICTORY

OKAY... THIS WAS INTERESTING!

Tomorrow's Intention:

DATE:

today's tiny victory

I AM VERY GRATEFUL FOR

①

②

③

THIS MADE ME SMILE

☺

TOMORROW'S
INTENTION:

Today's Tiny Victory:

DATE:

THIS WAS PRETTY COOL:

WOW!

I AM SUPER GRATEFUL FOR:

1

2

3

TOMORROW'S INTENTION

SO VERY GRATEFUL FOR:

1

2

3

DATE:

TODAY'S TINY VICTORY

This made me smile

Tomorrow's Intention:

Date:

Today I Am Grateful For:

1
2
3

TODAY'S tiny VICTORY

OKAY... THIS WAS INTERESTING!

Tomorrow's Intention:

DATE:

So Grateful Today For:

WELL, THIS WAS interesting!

Today's Tiny Victory:

TOMORROW'S INTENTION:

DATE:

So Grateful Today For:

①

②

③

Well, This Was Pretty AWESOME:

Today's Tiny Victory:

TOMORROW'S INTENTION:

DATE:

Today I Am Grateful For:

1

2

3

TODAY'S tiny VICTORY

OKAY... THIS WAS INTERESTING!

Tomorrow's Intention:

What If I...?*

* consider the possibilities!

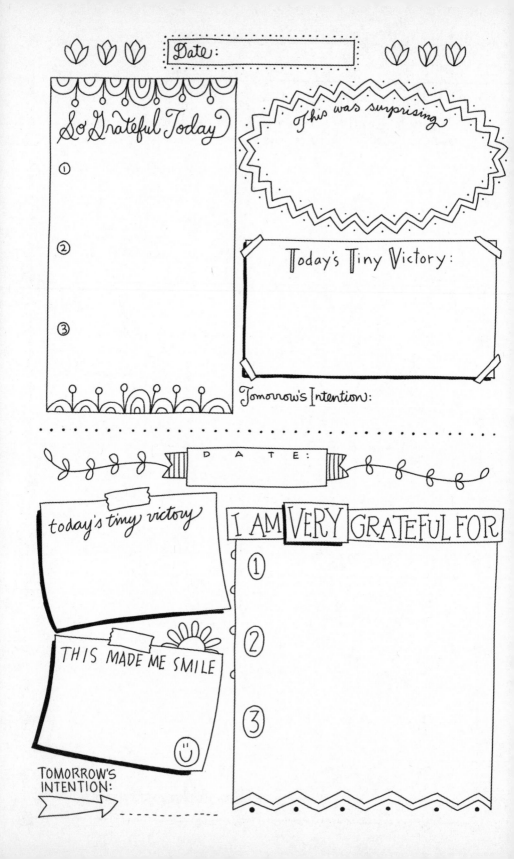

Date:

So Grateful Today

①

②

③

This was surprising

Today's Tiny Victory:

Tomorrow's Intention:

DATE:

today's tiny victory

THIS MADE ME SMILE

TOMORROW'S
INTENTION:

I AM VERY GRATEFUL FOR

①

②

③

Date:

So Grateful Today

①
②
③

This was surprising

Today's Tiny Victory:

Tomorrow's Intention:

Today's Tiny Victory:

WOW!
I AM SUPER GRATEFUL FOR:
1
2
3

DATE:

THIS WAS PRETTY COOL:

TOMORROW'S INTENTION

Date:

This made me smile:

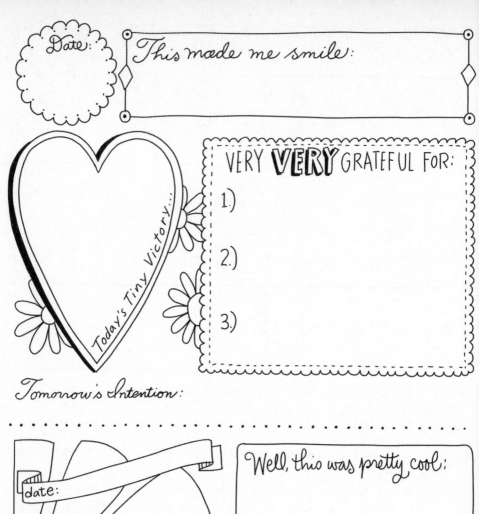

Today's Tiny Victory...

VERY **VERY** GRATEFUL FOR:

1.)

2.)

3.)

Tomorrow's Intention:

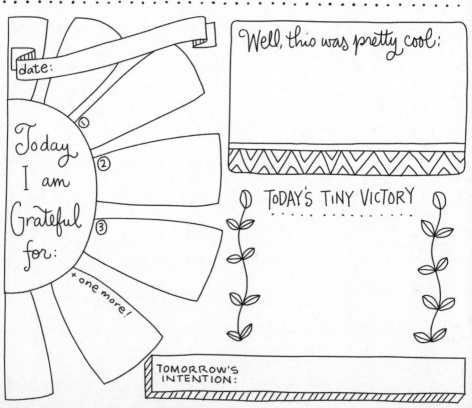

date:

Today I am Grateful for:

① ② ③

+ one more!

Well, this was pretty cool:

TODAY'S TINY VICTORY

TOMORROW'S INTENTION:

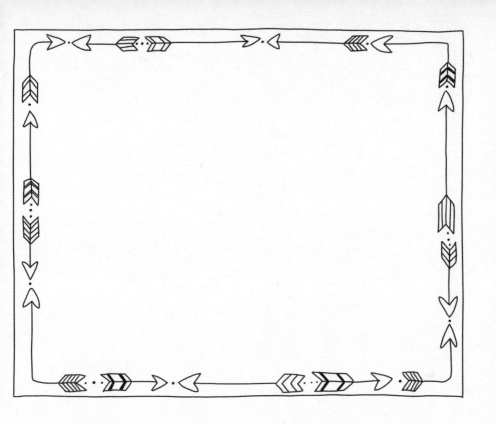

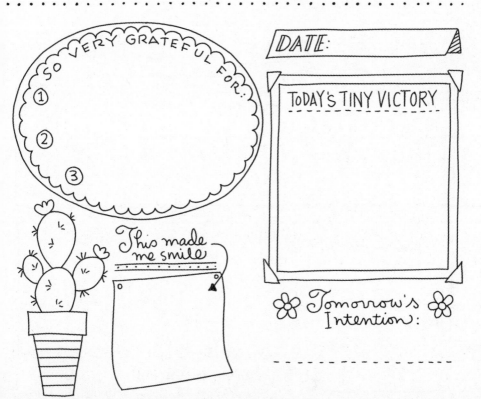

SO VERY GRATEFUL FOR...

1

2

3

DATE:

TODAY'S TINY VICTORY

This made me smile

Tomorrow's Intention:

DATE:

So very Grateful

1.
2.
3.

Today's Tiny Victory:

That Was Interesting!

tomorrow's intention:

- - - - - - - - - - - - - - - -

DATE:

So Grateful Today For:

WELL, THIS WAS interesting!

Today's Tiny Victory:

TOMORROW'S INTENTION:

Today's Tiny Victory:

WOW!

I AM SUPER GRATEFUL FOR:

1
2
3

DATE:

THIS WAS PRETTY COOL:

TOMORROW'S INTENTION

Date:

Today, I Am Grateful For:

1
2
3

TODAY'S tiny VICTORY

OKAY... THIS WAS INTERESTING!

Tomorrow's Intention:

Date:

So Grateful Today

①

②

③

This was surprising

Today's Tiny Victory:

Tomorrow's Intention:

my DREAMS

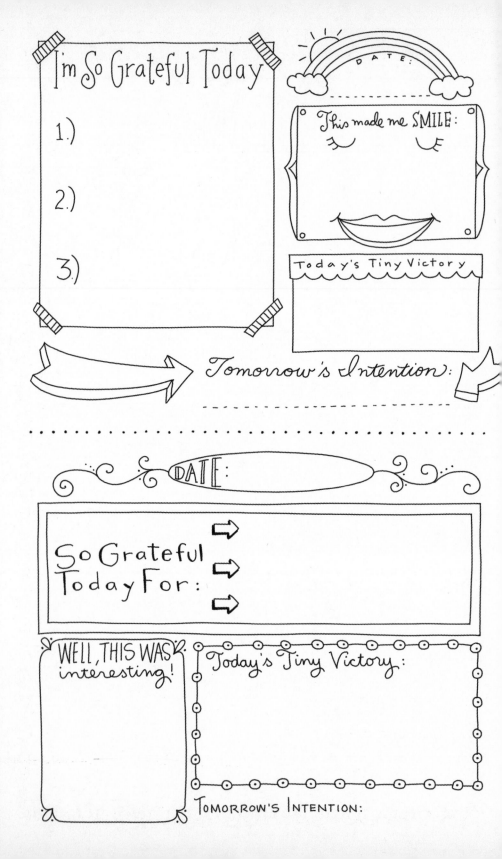

I'm So Grateful Today

1.)

2.)

3.)

DATE:

This made me SMILE:

Today's Tiny Victory

Tomorrow's Intention:

DATE:

So Grateful Today For:

WELL, THIS WAS interesting!

Today's Tiny Victory:

TOMORROW'S INTENTION:

DATE:

So Grateful Today For:

①

②

③

Well, This Was Pretty AWESOME:

Today's Tiny Victory:

TOMORROW'S INTENTION:

date:

VERY grateful for:

①

②

③

hmmm...this made me think today:

Today's Tiny Victory

TOMORROW'S INTENTION:

Today's Tiny Victory:

DATE:

THIS WAS PRETTY COOL:

WOW!

I AM SUPER GRATEFUL FOR:

1

2

3

TOMORROW'S INTENTION

DATE:

So very Grateful

1.

2.

3.

Today's Tiny Victory:

That Was Interesting!

tomorrow's intention:

Date:

This made me smile:

VERY **VERY** GRATEFUL FOR:

1.)

2.)

3.)

Today's Tiny Victory...

Tomorrow's Intention:

Date:

So Grateful Today

① ② ③

This was surprising

Today's Tiny Victory:

Tomorrow's Intention:

Today's Tiny Victory:

DATE:

THIS WAS PRETTY COOL:

WOW!

I AM SUPER GRATEFUL FOR:

1
2
3

TOMORROW'S INTENTION

DATE:

So very Grateful

1.
2.
3.

Today's Tiny Victory:

That Was Interesting!

tomorrow's intention:

Date:

This made me smile:

Today's Tiny Victory...

VERY **VERY** GRATEFUL FOR:

1.)

2.)

3.)

Tomorrow's Intention:

Date:

So Grateful Today

①

②

③

This was surprising

Today's Tiny Victory:

Tomorrow's Intention:

DATE:

So Grateful Today For:

①

②

③

Well, This Was Pretty AWESOME:

Today's Tiny Victory:

TOMORROW'S INTENTION:

Today's Tiny Victory:

WOW!
I AM SUPER GRATEFUL FOR:

1

2

3

DATE:

THIS WAS PRETTY COOL:

TOMORROW'S INTENTION

Date:

So Grateful Today

①

②

③

This was surprising

Today's Tiny Victory:

Tomorrow's Intention:

date:

Today I am Grateful for:

①
②
③
+ one more!

Well, this was pretty cool:

TODAY'S TINY VICTORY

TOMORROW'S INTENTION:

Date:

This made me smile:

Today's Tiny Victory...

VERY **VERY** GRATEFUL FOR:

1.)

2.)

3.)

Tomorrow's Intention:

Today's Tiny Victory:

DATE:

THIS WAS PRETTY COOL:

WOW!

I AM SUPER GRATEFUL FOR:

1

2

3

TOMORROW'S INTENTION

Date:

So Grateful Today

①

②

③

This was surprising

Today's Tiny Victory:

Tomorrow's Intention:

...AND ANOTHER THING!

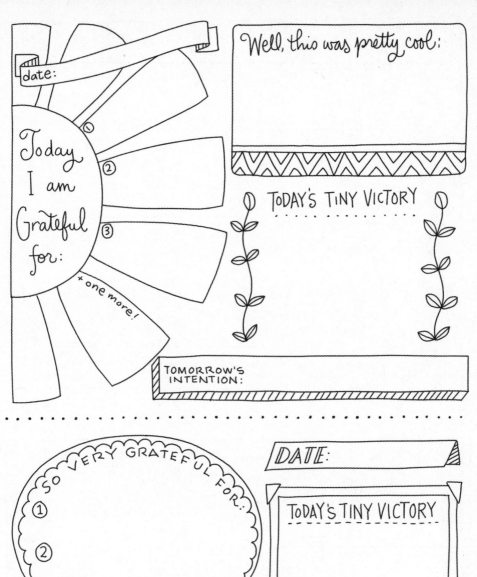

date:

Today I am Grateful for:

① ② ③

+ one more!

Well, this was pretty cool:

TODAY'S TINY VICTORY

TOMORROW'S INTENTION:

SO VERY GRATEFUL FOR:

① ② ③

This made me smile

DATE:

TODAY'S TINY VICTORY

Tomorrow's Intention:

DATE:

So very Grateful

1.

2.

3.

Today's Tiny Victory:

That Was Interesting!

tomorrow's intention:
- - - - - - - - - - - - - -

· ·

Date:

Today I Am Grateful For:

[1]

[2]

[3]

TODAY'S tiny VICTORY

OKAY... THIS WAS INTERESTING!

Tomorrow's Intention:

DATE:

today's tiny victory

THIS MADE ME SMILE

TOMORROW'S
INTENTION:

I AM VERY GRATEFUL FOR

①

②

③

Today's Tiny Victory:

DATE:

THIS WAS PRETTY COOL:

WOW!

I AM SUPER GRATEFUL FOR:

1
2
3

TOMORROW'S INTENTION

SO VERY GRATEFUL FOR:

1
2
3

DATE:

TODAY'S TINY VICTORY

This made me smile

Tomorrow's Intention:

DATE:

So Grateful Today For:

WELL, THIS WAS interesting!

Today's Tiny Victory:

TOMORROW'S INTENTION:

DATE:

So Grateful Today For:

①

②

③

Well, This Was Pretty AWESOME:

Today's Tiny Victory:

TOMORROW'S INTENTION:

DATE:

Today I Am Grateful For:

1

2

3

TODAY'S tiny VICTORY

OKAY... THIS WAS INTERESTING!

Tomorrow's Intention:

What If I... ?*

....

....

....

....

....

....

....

....

....

....

....

....

* consider the possibilities!

Date:

So Grateful Today
①
②
③

This was surprising

Today's Tiny Victory:

Tomorrow's Intention:

D A T E:

today's tiny victory

THIS MADE ME SMILE

I AM VERY GRATEFUL FOR
①
②
③

TOMORROW'S
INTENTION:

Date:

So Grateful Today
①
②
③

This was surprising

Today's Tiny Victory:

Tomorrow's Intention:

Today's Tiny Victory:

DATE:

THIS WAS PRETTY COOL:

WOW!

I AM SUPER GRATEFUL FOR:
1
2
3

TOMORROW'S INTENTION

Date:

This made me smile:

Today's Tiny Victory...

VERY **VERY** GRATEFUL FOR:

1.)

2.)

3.)

Tomorrow's Intention:

date:

Today I am Grateful for:

① ② ③

+ one more!

Well, this was pretty cool:

TODAY'S TINY VICTORY

TOMORROW'S INTENTION:

DATE:

So Grateful Today For: ⇨ ⇨ ⇨

WELL, THIS WAS interesting!

Today's Tiny Victory:

TOMORROW'S INTENTION:

SO VERY GRATEFUL FOR...
① ② ③

This made me smile

DATE:

TODAY'S TINY VICTORY

❀ Tomorrow's ❀ Intention:

DATE:

So very Grateful

1.

2.

3.

Today's Tiny Victory:

That Was Interesting!

tomorrow's intention:

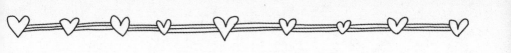

Date:

Today, I Am Grateful For:

1

2

3

TODAY'S
tiny
VICTORY

OKAY... THIS WAS INTERESTING!

Tomorrow's
Intention:

Today's Tiny Victory:

DATE:

THIS WAS PRETTY COOL:

WOW!

I AM SUPER GRATEFUL FOR:

1

2

3

TOMORROW'S INTENTION

Date:

So Grateful Today

①

②

③

This was surprising

Today's Tiny Victory:

Tomorrow's Intention:

Lately I've been thinking...

I'm So Grateful Today

1.)

2.)

3.)

DATE:

This made me SMILE:

Today's Tiny Victory

Tomorrow's Intention:

- -

DATE:

So Grateful Today For:

WELL, THIS WAS interesting!

Today's Tiny Victory:

TOMORROW'S INTENTION:

DATE:

So Grateful
Today For:

①
②
③

Well, This Was Pretty
AWESOME:

Today's Tiny Victory:

TOMORROW'S INTENTION:

date:

VERY grateful
for:

①
②
③

hmmm...this made me think today:

Today's Tiny Victory

TOMORROW'S INTENTION:

Today's Tiny Victory:

DATE:

THIS WAS PRETTY COOL:

WOW!

I AM SUPER GRATEFUL FOR:

1

2

3

TOMORROW'S INTENTION

DATE:

So very Grateful

1.

2.

3.

Today's Tiny Victory:

That Was Interesting!

tomorrow's intention:

Date:

This made me smile:

Today's Tiny Victory...

VERY **VERY** GRATEFUL FOR:

1.)

2.)

3.)

Tomorrow's Intention:

SO VERY GRATEFUL FOR:

① ② ③

This made me smile

DATE:

TODAY'S TINY VICTORY

✿ Tomorrow's Intention: ✿

- - - - - - - - - - - - - - - -

Date:

So Grateful Today

① ② ③

This was surprising

Today's Tiny Victory:

Tomorrow's Intention:

date:

hmmm...this made me think today.

VERY grateful for:

1

2

3

Today's Tiny Victory

TOMORROW'S INTENTION:

date:

Today I Am Grateful For:

1

2

3

TODAY'S tiny VICTORY

OKAY... THIS WAS INTERESTING!

Tomorrow's Intention:

I'm So Grateful Today

1.)

2.)

3.)

DATE:

This made me SMILE:

Today's Tiny Victory

Tomorrow's Intention:

Today's Tiny Victory:

DATE:

THIS WAS PRETTY COOL:

WOW!

I AM SUPER GRATEFUL FOR:

1

2

3

TOMORROW'S INTENTION

Date:

This made me smile:

Today's Tiny Intention...

VERY **VERY** GRATEFUL FOR:

1.)

2.)

3.)

Tomorrow's Intention:

· ·

Today's Tiny Victory:

DATE:

THIS WAS PRETTY COOL:

WOW!

I AM SUPER GRATEFUL FOR:

 1

 2

3

TOMORROW'S INTENTION

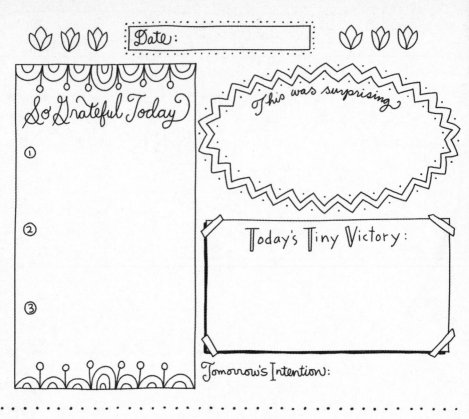

Date:

So Grateful Today

①

②

③

This was surprising

Today's Tiny Victory:

Tomorrow's Intention:

my DREAMS

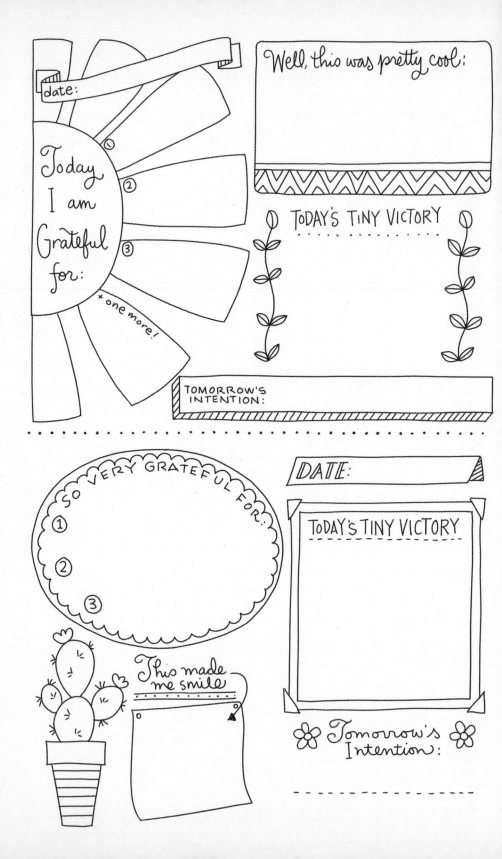

DATE:

So very Grateful

1.

2.

3.

Today's Tiny Victory:

That Was Interesting!

tomorrow's intention:

Date:

Today, I Am Grateful For:

1

2

3

TODAY'S tiny VICTORY

OKAY... THIS WAS INTERESTING!

Tomorrow's Intention:

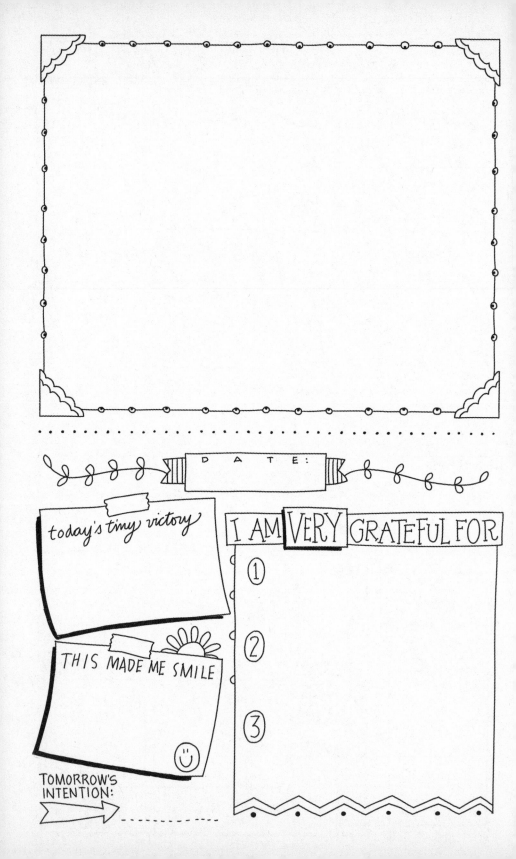

DATE:

today's tiny victory

I AM VERY GRATEFUL FOR

THIS MADE ME SMILE

①

②

③

TOMORROW'S
INTENTION:

DATE:

So very Grateful →

1.

2.

3.

Today's Tiny Victory:

That Was Interesting!

tomorrow's intention:

- -

Date:

So Grateful Today

①

②

③

This was surprising

Today's Tiny Victory:

Tomorrow's Intention:

So grateful for these *PEOPLE!

*super amazing

Date:

This made me smile:

Today's Tiny Victory...

VERY **VERY** GRATEFUL FOR:

1.)

2.)

3.)

Tomorrow's Intention:

DATE:

So Grateful Today For:

WELL, THIS WAS interesting!

Today's Tiny Victory:

TOMORROW'S INTENTION:

DATE:

So Grateful Today For:

1

2

3

Well, This Was Pretty AWESOME:

Today's Tiny Victory:

TOMORROW'S INTENTION:

Date:

This made me smile:

Today's Tiny Victory...

VERY **VERY** GRATEFUL FOR:

1.)

2.)

3.)

Tomorrow's Intention:

Today's Tiny Victory:

DATE:

THIS WAS PRETTY COOL:

WOW!

I AM SUPER GRATEFUL FOR:

1

2

3

TOMORROW'S INTENTION

Date: _____

So Grateful Today

① _____

② _____

③ _____

This was surprising

Today's Tiny Victory:

Tomorrow's Intention:

my DREAMS

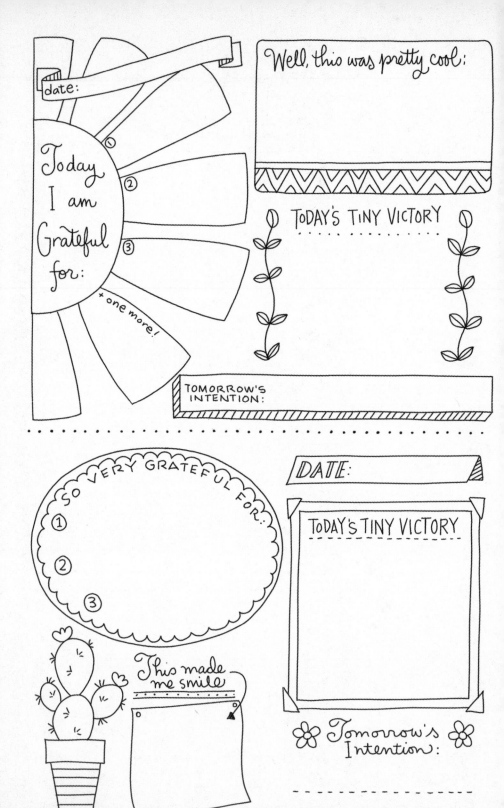

date:

Today I am Grateful for:

① ② ③

+ one more!

Well, this was pretty cool:

TODAY'S TINY VICTORY

TOMORROW'S INTENTION:

SO VERY GRATEFUL FOR..

① ② ③

This made me smile

DATE:

TODAY'S TINY VICTORY

Tomorrow's Intention:

DATE:

So very Grateful

1.

2.

3.

Today's Tiny Victory:

That Was Interesting!

tomorrow's intention:

Date:

Today I Am Grateful For:

1

2

3

TODAY'S tiny VICTORY

OKAY... THIS WAS INTERESTING!

Tomorrow's Intention:

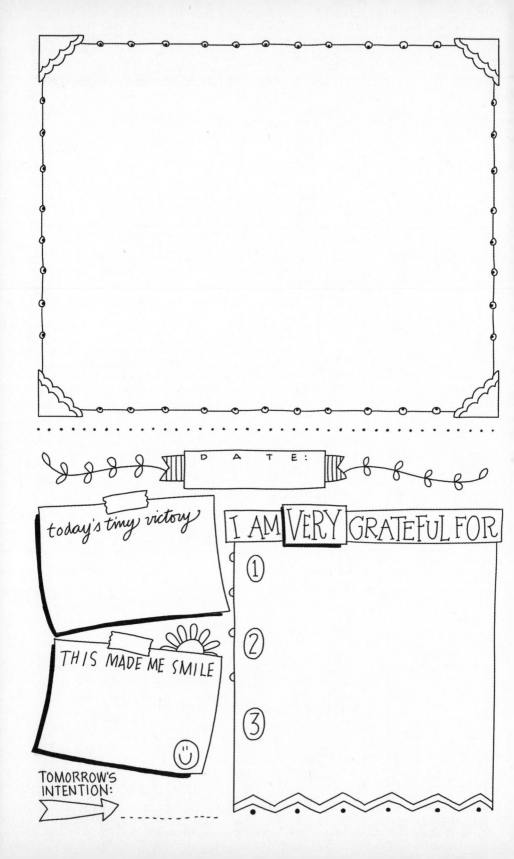

DATE:

today's tiny victory

THIS MADE ME SMILE

TOMORROW'S
INTENTION:

I AM VERY GRATEFUL FOR

①

②

③

date:

hmmm...this made me think today:

VERY grateful for:

1

2

3

Today's Tiny Victory

TOMORROW'S INTENTION:

I'm So Grateful Today

1.)

2.)

3.)

DATE:

This made me SMILE:

Today's Tiny Victory

Tomorrow's Intention:

Today's Tiny Victory:

DATE:

THIS WAS PRETTY COOL:

WOW!

I AM SUPER GRATEFUL FOR:

1

2

3

TOMORROW'S INTENTION

SO VERY GRATEFUL FOR:

① ② ③

DATE:

TODAY'S TINY VICTORY

This made me smile

❀ Tomorrow's Intention: ❀

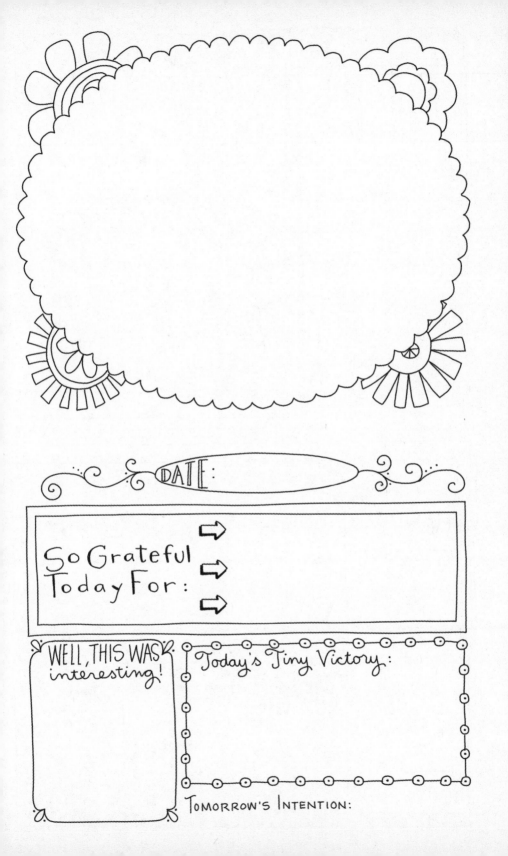

DATE:

So Grateful Today For:

WELL, THIS WAS interesting!

Today's Tiny Victory:

TOMORROW'S INTENTION:

DATE:

So Grateful Today For:

1

2

3

Well, This Was Pretty AWESOME:

Today's Tiny Victory:

TOMORROW'S INTENTION:

Date:

TODAY'S tiny VICTORY

Today I Am Grateful For:

1

2

3

OKAY... THIS WAS INTERESTING!

Tomorrow's Intention:

What If I... ?*

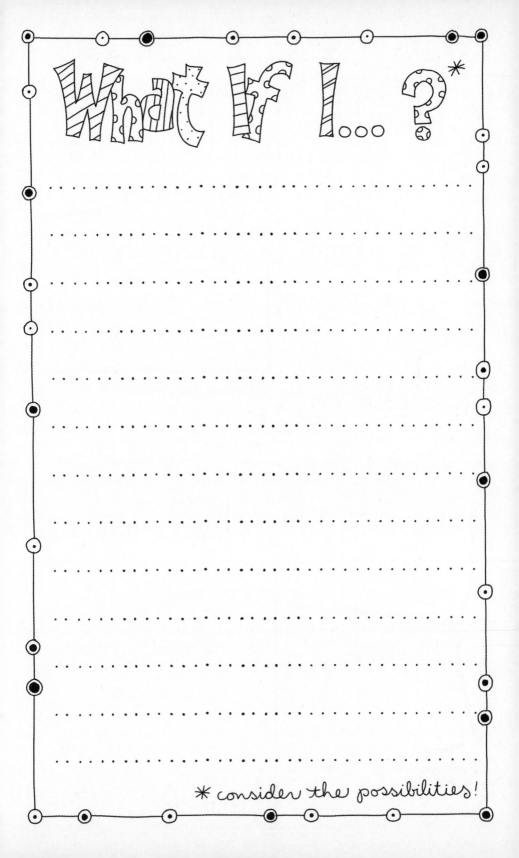

. . . .

. . . .

. . . .

. . . .

. . . .

. . . .

. . . .

. . . .

. . . .

. . . .

. . . .

* consider the possibilities!

Date:

So Grateful Today

①

②

③

This was surprising

Today's Tiny Victory:

Tomorrow's Intention:

D A T E :

today's tiny victory

I AM VERY GRATEFUL FOR

①

②

③

THIS MADE ME SMILE

TOMORROW'S
INTENTION:

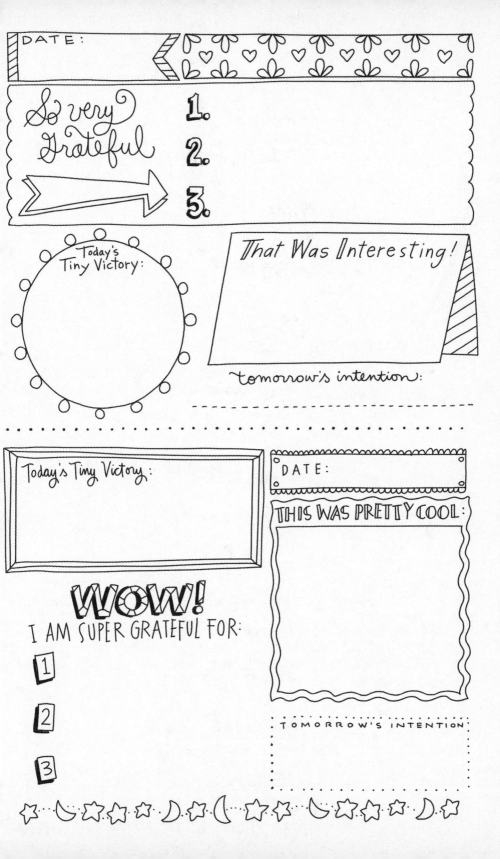

DATE:

So very Grateful

1.
2.
3.

Today's Tiny Victory:

That Was Interesting!

tomorrow's intention:

Today's Tiny Victory:

DATE:

THIS WAS PRETTY COOL:

WOW!
I AM SUPER GRATEFUL FOR:

1
2
3

TOMORROW'S INTENTION

Date:

This made me smile:

Today's Tiny Victory...

VERY **VERY** GRATEFUL FOR:

1.)

2.)

3.)

Tomorrow's Intention:

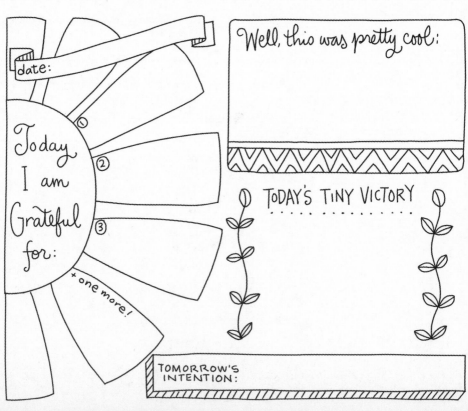

date:

Today I am Grateful for:

① ② ③

+ one more!

Well, this was pretty cool:

TODAY'S TINY VICTORY

TOMORROW'S INTENTION:

SO VERY GRATEFUL FOR...

①
②
③

This made me smile

DATE:

TODAY'S TINY VICTORY

❀ Tomorrow's ❀ Intention:

Date:

So Grateful Today

①

②

③

This was surprising

Today's Tiny Victory:

Tomorrow's Intention:

Lately I've been thinking...

I'm So Grateful Today

DATE:

1.)

2.)

3.)

This made me SMILE:

Today's Tiny Victory

Tomorrow's Intention:

DATE:

So Grateful Today For:

WELL, THIS WAS interesting!

Today's Tiny Victory:

TOMORROW'S INTENTION:

DATE:

So Grateful Today For:

①

②

③

Well, This Was Pretty AWESOME:

Today's Tiny Victory:

TOMORROW'S INTENTION:

date:

VERY grateful for:

1

2

3

hmmm...this made me think today:

Today's Tiny Victory

TOMORROW'S INTENTION:

Today's Tiny Victory:

DATE:

THIS WAS PRETTY COOL:

WOW!

I AM SUPER GRATEFUL FOR:

1

2

3

TOMORROW'S INTENTION

DATE:

So very Grateful

1.

2.

3.

Today's Tiny Victory:

That Was Interesting!

tomorrow's intention:

Date:

This made me smile:

Today's Tiny Victory...

VERY **VERY** GRATEFUL FOR:

1.)

2.)

3.)

Tomorrow's Intention:

Date:

So Grateful Today

①

②

③

This was surprising

Today's Tiny Victory:

Tomorrow's Intention:

SO VERY GRATEFUL FOR...

①

②

③

This made
me smile

DATE:

TODAY'S TINY VICTORY

❀ Tomorrow's ❀
   Intention:

- - - - - - - - - - - - - -

date:

VERY grateful for:

1

2

3

hmmm...this made me think today.

Today's Tiny Victory

TOMORROW'S INTENTION:

I'm So Grateful Today

1.)

2.)

3.)

DATE:

This made me SMILE:

Today's Tiny Victory

Tomorrow's Intention:

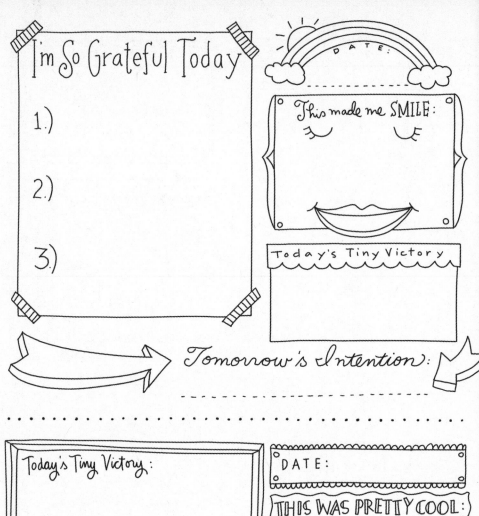

I'm So Grateful Today

1.)

2.)

3.)

DATE:

This made me SMILE:

Today's Tiny Victory

Tomorrow's Intention:

Today's Tiny Victory:

DATE:

THIS WAS PRETTY COOL:

WOW!

I AM SUPER GRATEFUL FOR:

1

2

3

TOMORROW'S INTENTION

Date:

So Grateful Today

①

②

③

This was surprising

Today's Tiny Victory:

Tomorrow's Intention:

date:

Today I am Grateful for:

①
②
③

+ one more!

Well, this was pretty cool:

TODAY'S TINY VICTORY

TOMORROW'S INTENTION:

Date:

This made me smile:

Today's Tiny Victory...

VERY **VERY** GRATEFUL FOR:

1.)

2.)

3.)

Tomorrow's Intention:

Today's Tiny Victory:

DATE:

THIS WAS PRETTY COOL:

WOW!

I AM SUPER GRATEFUL FOR:

1

2

3

TOMORROW'S INTENTION

Date: _____

So Grateful Today

① _____

② _____

③ _____

This was surprising

Today's Tiny Victory:

Tomorrow's Intention:

Ideas...IDEAS... Ideas...ideas...IDEAS

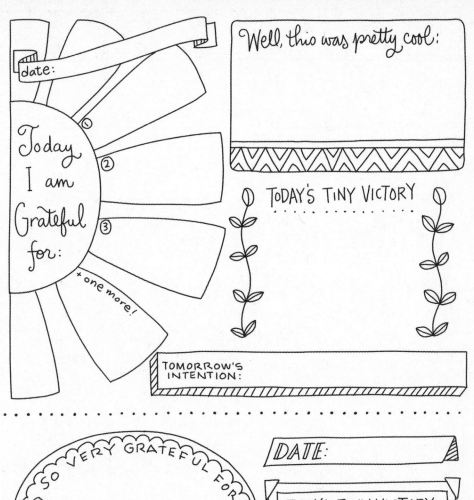

date:

Today I am Grateful for:

① ② ③ + one more!

Well, this was pretty cool:

TODAY'S TINY VICTORY

TOMORROW'S INTENTION:

SO VERY GRATEFUL FOR:

① ② ③

This made me smile

DATE:

TODAY'S TINY VICTORY

Tomorrow's Intention:

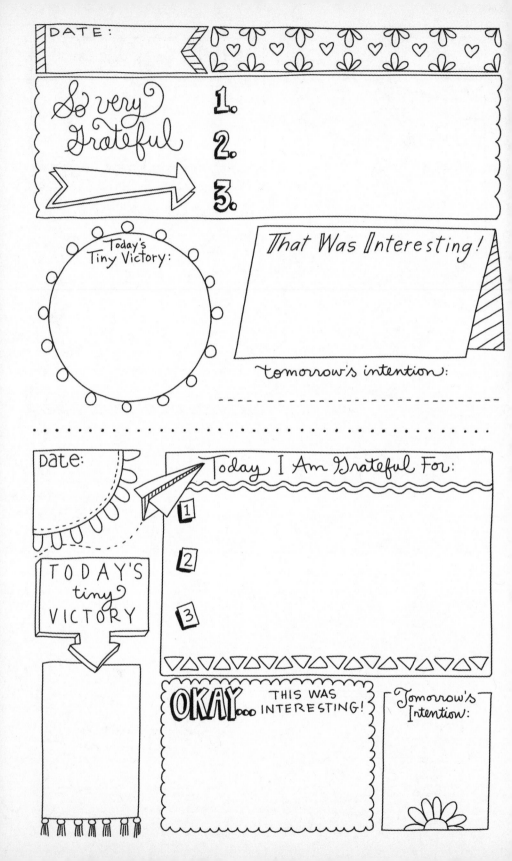

DATE:

So very Grateful

1.

2.

3.

Today's Tiny Victory:

That Was Interesting!

tomorrow's intention:

- - - - - - - - - - - - - -

Date:

Today I Am Grateful For:

1

2

3

TODAY'S tiny VICTORY

OKAY... THIS WAS INTERESTING!

Tomorrow's Intention:

D A T E :

today's tiny victory

THIS MADE ME SMILE

I AM VERY GRATEFUL FOR

①

②

③

TOMORROW'S
INTENTION:

Date:

Today, I Am Grateful For:

1
2
3

TODAY'S tiny VICTORY

OKAY... THIS WAS INTERESTING!

Tomorrow's Intention:

DATE:

So Grateful Today For:

WELL, THIS WAS interesting!

Today's Tiny Victory:

TOMORROW'S INTENTION:

DATE:

So Grateful Today For:

①

②

③

Well, This Was Pretty AWESOME:

Today's Tiny Victory:

TOMORROW'S INTENTION:

DATE:

Today, I Am Grateful For:

①

②

③

TODAY'S tiny VICTORY

OKAY... THIS WAS INTERESTING!

Tomorrow's Intention:

What If I... ?*

....
....
....
....
....
....
....
....
....
....
....
....

* consider the possibilities!

Date:

So Grateful Today

①

②

③

This was surprising

Today's Tiny Victory:

Tomorrow's Intention:

D A T E:

today's tiny victory

THIS MADE ME SMILE

TOMORROW'S INTENTION:

I AM VERY GRATEFUL FOR

①

②

③

Date:

So Grateful Today

①

②

③

This was surprising

Today's Tiny Victory:

Tomorrow's Intention:

Today's Tiny Victory:

WOW!
I AM SUPER GRATEFUL FOR:

1

2

3

DATE:

THIS WAS PRETTY COOL:

TOMORROW'S INTENTION

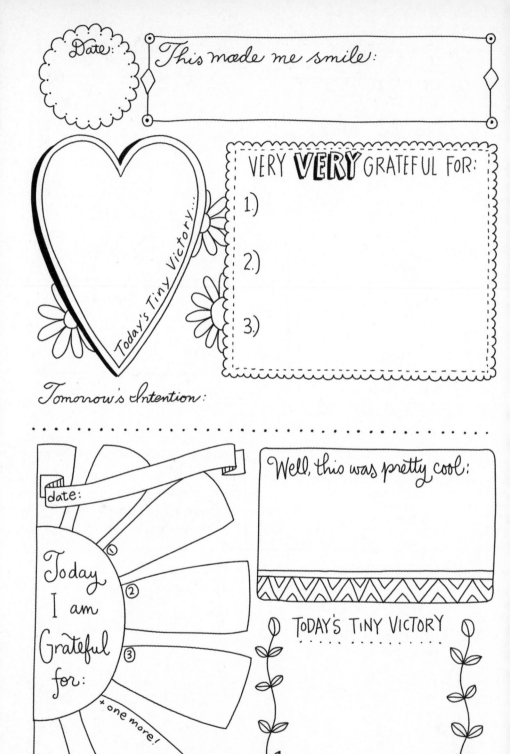

Date:

This made me smile:

Today's Tiny Victory...

VERY **VERY** GRATEFUL FOR:

1.)

2.)

3.)

Tomorrow's Intention:

date:

Today I am Grateful for:

① ② ③

+ one more!

Well, this was pretty cool:

TODAY'S TINY VICTORY

TOMORROW'S INTENTION:

SO VERY GRATEFUL FOR...

①

②

③

This made me smile

DATE:

TODAY'S TINY VICTORY

Tomorrow's Intention:

DATE:

So very Grateful

1.

2.

3.

Today's Tiny Victory:

That Was Interesting!

tomorrow's intention:
- - - - - - - - - - - - - - - - - - -

. . . .

DATE:

So Grateful Today For:

WELL, THIS WAS interesting!

Today's Tiny Victory:

TOMORROW'S INTENTION:

Today's Tiny Victory:

WOW!

I AM SUPER GRATEFUL FOR:

1

2

3

DATE:

THIS WAS PRETTY COOL:

TOMORROW'S INTENTION

Date:

Today I Am Grateful For:

1

2

3

TODAY'S tiny VICTORY

OKAY... THIS WAS INTERESTING!

Tomorrow's Intention:

Date:

So Grateful Today

①

②

③

This was surprising

Today's Tiny Victory:

Tomorrow's Intention:

my DREAMS

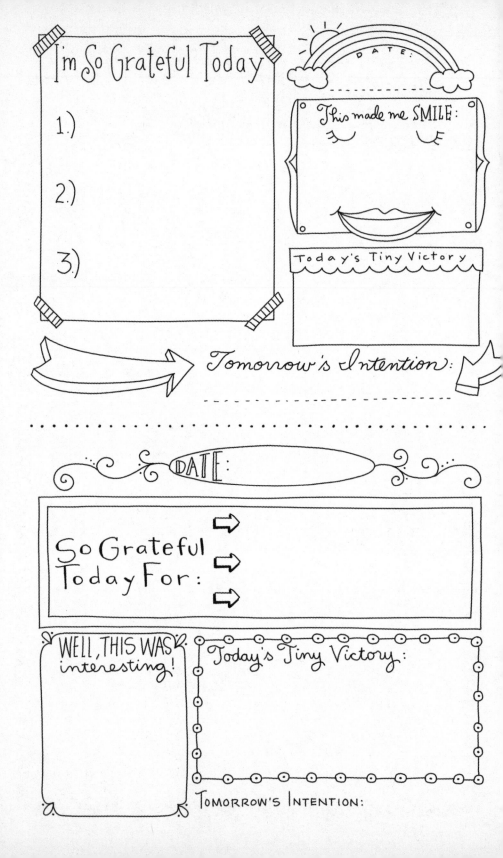

I'm So Grateful Today

1.)

2.)

3.)

DATE:

This made me SMILE:

Today's Tiny Victory

Tomorrow's Intention:

DATE:

So Grateful Today For:

WELL, THIS WAS interesting!

Today's Tiny Victory:

TOMORROW'S INTENTION:

DATE:

So Grateful Today For:

①

②

③

Well, This Was Pretty AWESOME:

Today's Tiny Victory:

TOMORROW'S INTENTION:

date:

VERY grateful for:

①

②

③

hmmm...this made me think today.

Today's Tiny Victory

TOMORROW'S INTENTION:

Today's Tiny Victory:

DATE:

THIS WAS PRETTY COOL:

WOW!

I AM SUPER GRATEFUL FOR:

1

2

3

TOMORROW'S INTENTION

DATE:

So very Grateful

1.

2.

3.

Today's Tiny Victory:

That Was Interesting!

tomorrow's intention:

Date:

This made me smile:

Today's Tiny Victory...

VERY **VERY** GRATEFUL FOR:

1.)

2.)

3.)

Tomorrow's Intention:

Date:

So Grateful Today

① ② ③

This was surprising

Today's Tiny Victory:

Tomorrow's Intention:

Date:

This made me smile:

Today's Tiny Victory...

VERY **VERY** GRATEFUL FOR:

1.)

2.)

3.)

Tomorrow's Intention:

Date:

So Grateful Today

①

②

③

This was surprising

Today's Tiny Victory:

Tomorrow's Intention:

DATE:

So Grateful Today For:

1

2

3

Well, This Was Pretty AWESOME:

Today's Tiny Victory

TOMORROW'S INTENTION:

Today's Tiny Victory:

WOW!
I AM SUPER GRATEFUL FOR:

1

2

3

DATE:

THIS WAS PRETTY COOL:

TOMORROW'S INTENTION

Date:

So Grateful Today

①

②

③

This was surprising

Today's Tiny Victory:

Tomorrow's Intention:

date:

Today I am Grateful for:

①
②
③

+ one more!

Well, this was pretty cool:

TODAY'S TINY VICTORY

TOMORROW'S INTENTION:

Date:

This made me smile:

Today's Tiny Victory...

VERY **VERY** GRATEFUL FOR:

1.)

2.)

3.)

Tomorrow's Intention:

Today's Tiny Victory:

DATE:

THIS WAS PRETTY COOL:

WOW!

I AM SUPER GRATEFUL FOR:

1

2

3

TOMORROW'S INTENTION

Date:

So Grateful Today

①

②

③

This was surprising

Today's Tiny Victory:

Tomorrow's Intention:

...AND ANOTHER THING!

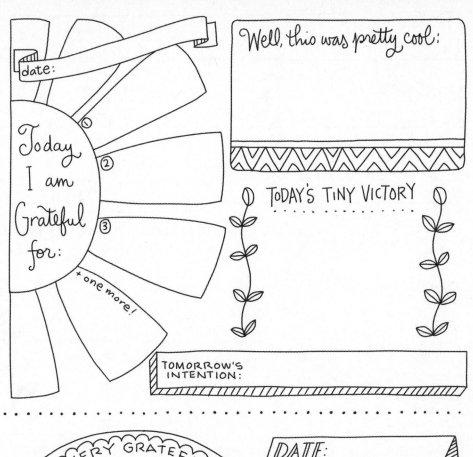

date:

Today I am Grateful for:

① ② ③ + one more!

Well, this was pretty cool:

TODAY'S TINY VICTORY

TOMORROW'S INTENTION:

SO VERY GRATEFUL FOR:

① ② ③

This made me smile

DATE:

TODAY'S TINY VICTORY

Tomorrow's Intention:

DATE:

So very Grateful

1.

2.

3.

Today's Tiny Victory:

That Was Interesting!

tomorrow's intention:

- -

Date:

Today I Am Grateful For:

1

2

3

TODAY'S tiny VICTORY

OKAY... THIS WAS INTERESTING!

Tomorrow's Intention:

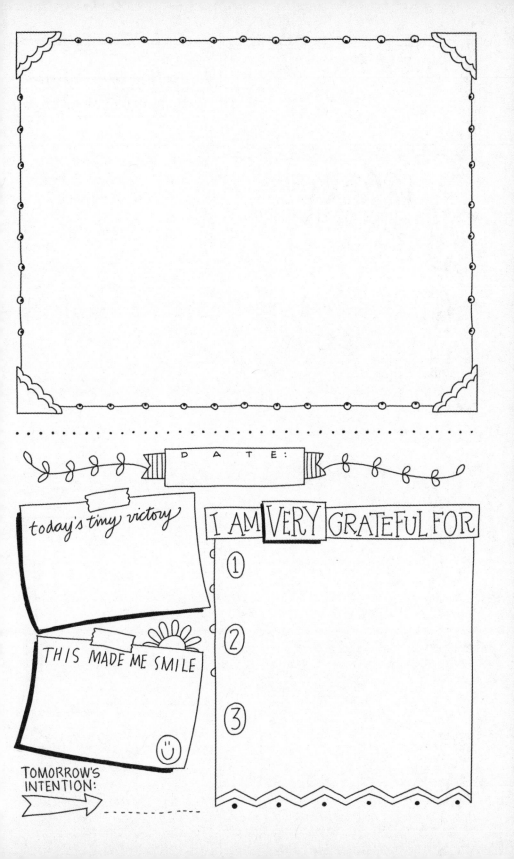

DATE:

today's tiny victory

THIS MADE ME SMILE

TOMORROW'S
INTENTION:

I AM VERY GRATEFUL FOR

①

②

③

Today's Tiny Victory:

WOW!

I AM SUPER GRATEFUL FOR:

1

2

3

DATE:

THIS WAS PRETTY COOL:

TOMORROW'S INTENTION

SO VERY GRATEFUL FOR...

1

2

3

This made me smile

DATE:

TODAY'S TINY VICTORY

Tomorrow's Intention:

DATE:

So Grateful Today For: ⇨ ⇨ ⇨

WELL, THIS WAS interesting!

Today's Tiny Victory:

Tomorrow's Intention:

DATE:

So Grateful Today For:

① ② ③

Well, This Was Pretty AWESOME:

Today's Tiny Victory:

TOMORROW'S INTENTION:

DATE:

Today I Am Grateful For:

1 2 3

TODAY'S tiny VICTORY

OKAY... THIS WAS INTERESTING!

Tomorrow's Intention:

What If I... ?*

. . . .

. . . .

. . . .

. . . .

. . . .

. . . .

. . . .

. . . .

. . . .

. . . .

. . . .

. . . .

* consider the possibilities!

Date:

So Grateful Today

①

②

③

This was surprising

Today's Tiny Victory:

Tomorrow's Intention:

DATE:

today's tiny victory

THIS MADE ME SMILE

TOMORROW'S INTENTION:

I AM VERY GRATEFUL FOR

①

②

③

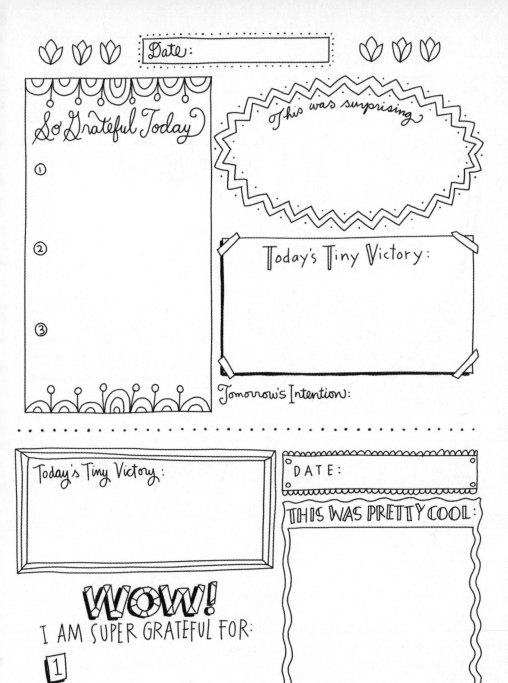

Date:

So Grateful Today

①

②

③

This was surprising

Today's Tiny Victory:

Tomorrow's Intention:

Today's Tiny Victory:

WOW!
I AM SUPER GRATEFUL FOR:

1

2

3

DATE:

THIS WAS PRETTY COOL:

TOMORROW'S INTENTION

Date:

This made me smile:

Today's Tiny Victory...

VERY **VERY** GRATEFUL FOR:

1.)

2.)

3.)

Tomorrow's Intention:

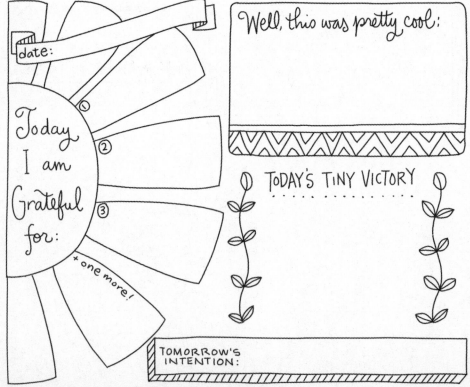

date:

Today I am Grateful for:

① ② ③

+ one more!

Well, this was pretty cool:

TODAY'S TINY VICTORY

TOMORROW'S INTENTION:

DATE:

So Grateful Today For: ⇒ ⇒ ⇒

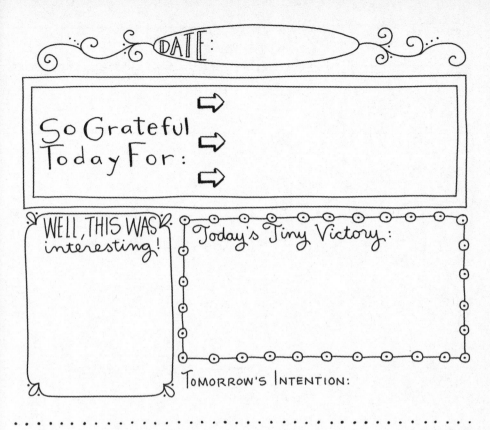

WELL, THIS WAS interesting!

Today's Tiny Victory:

Tomorrow's Intention:

SO VERY GRATEFUL FOR:
①
②
③

This made me smile

DATE:

TODAY'S TINY VICTORY

❀ Tomorrow's ❀ Intention:

DATE:

So very Grateful

1.

2.

3.

Today's Tiny Victory:

That Was Interesting!

tomorrow's intention:

- -

Date:

Today I Am Grateful For:

1

2

3

TODAY'S tiny VICTORY

OKAY... THIS WAS INTERESTING!

Tomorrow's Intention:

Today's Tiny Victory:

DATE:

THIS WAS PRETTY COOL:

WOW!

I AM SUPER GRATEFUL FOR:

1

2

3

TOMORROW'S INTENTION

Date:

So Grateful Today

① ② ③

This was surprising

Today's Tiny Victory:

Tomorrow's Intention:

Lately I've been thinking...

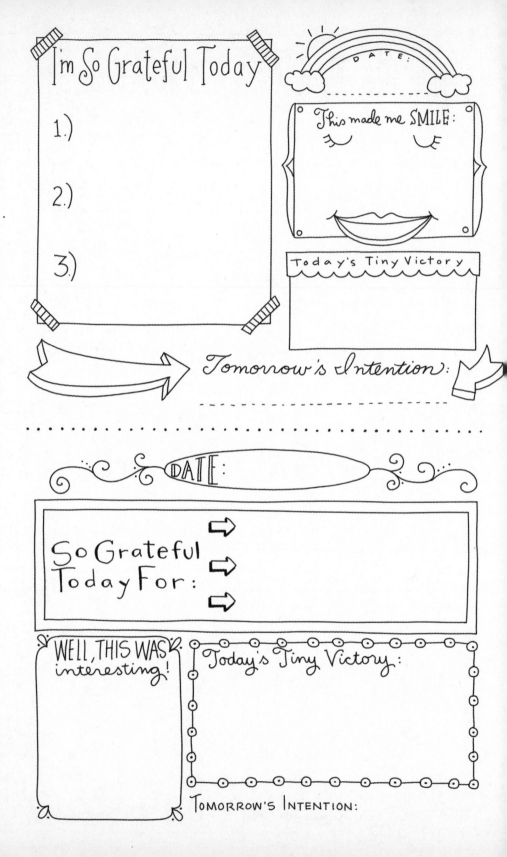

I'm So Grateful Today

DATE:

1.)

2.)

3.)

This made me SMILE:

Today's Tiny Victory

Tomorrow's Intention:

DATE:

So Grateful Today For:

WELL, THIS WAS interesting!

Today's Tiny Victory:

TOMORROW'S INTENTION:

DATE:

So Grateful Today For:

1
2
3

Well, This Was Pretty AWESOME:

Today's Tiny Victory:

TOMORROW'S INTENTION:

date:

VERY grateful for:

1
2
3

hmmm...this made me think today:

Today's Tiny Victory

TOMORROW'S INTENTION:

Today's Tiny Victory:

DATE:

THIS WAS PRETTY COOL:

WOW!
I AM SUPER GRATEFUL FOR:
1
2
3

TOMORROW'S INTENTION

DATE:

So very Grateful

1.
2.
3.

Today's Tiny Victory:

That Was Interesting!

tomorrow's intention:

Date:

This made me smile:

Today's Tiny Victory...

VERY **VERY** GRATEFUL FOR:

1.)

2.)

3.)

Tomorrow's Intention:

SO VERY GRATEFUL FOR..

①
②
③

This made me smile

DATE:

TODAY'S TINY VICTORY

❀ Tomorrow's Intention: ❀

Date:

So Grateful Today

①
②
③

This was surprising

Today's Tiny Victory:

Tomorrow's Intention:

date:

VERY grateful for:

① 1

② 2

③ 3

hmmm...this made me think today:

Today's Tiny Victory

TOMORROW'S INTENTION:

Date:

Today I Am Grateful For:

1
2
3

TODAY'S tiny VICTORY

OKAY... THIS WAS INTERESTING!

Tomorrow's Intention:

I'm So Grateful Today

1.)

2.)

3.)

DATE:

This made me SMILE:

Today's Tiny Victory

Tomorrow's Intention:

Today's Tiny Victory:

DATE:

THIS WAS PRETTY COOL:

WOW!

I AM SUPER GRATEFUL FOR:

1

2

3

TOMORROW'S INTENTION

Date:

This made me smile:

Today's Tiny Victory...

VERY **VERY** GRATEFUL FOR:

1.)

2.)

3.)

Tomorrow's Intention:

Today's Tiny Victory:

DATE:

THIS WAS PRETTY COOL:

WOW!

I AM SUPER GRATEFUL FOR:

 1

 2

 3

TOMORROW'S INTENTION

Date:

So Grateful Today

①

②

③

This was surprising

Today's Tiny Victory:

Tomorrow's Intention:

my DREAMS

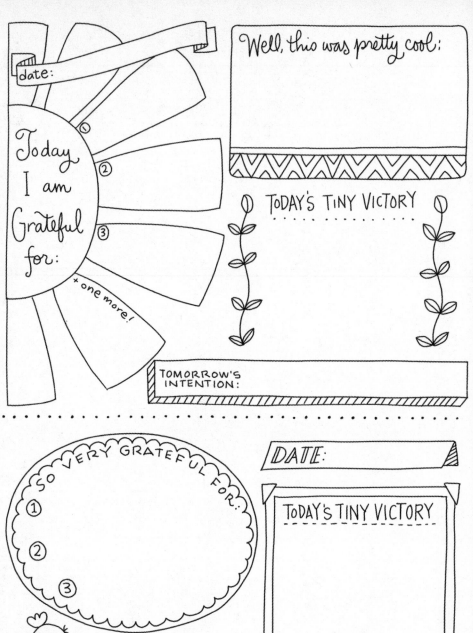

date:

Today I am Grateful for:

① ② ③

+ one more!

Well, this was pretty cool:

TODAY'S TINY VICTORY

TOMORROW'S INTENTION:

SO VERY GRATEFUL FOR:

① ② ③

This made me smile

DATE:

TODAY'S TINY VICTORY

❀ Tomorrow's ❀ Intention:

DATE:

So very Grateful

1.

2.

3.

Today's Tiny Victory:

That Was Interesting!

tomorrow's intention:

- -

Date:

Today I Am Grateful For:

1

2

3

TODAY'S tiny VICTORY

OKAY... THIS WAS INTERESTING!

Tomorrow's Intention:

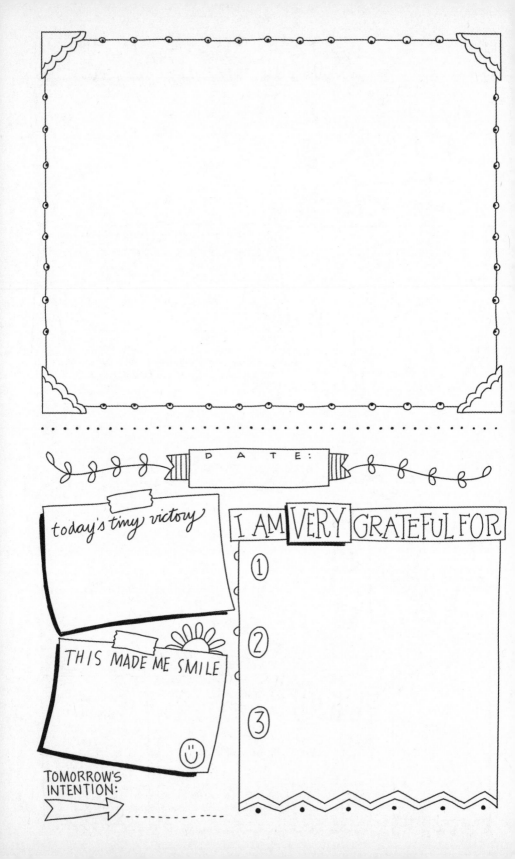

D A T E:

today's tiny victory

I AM VERY GRATEFUL FOR

①

②

③

THIS MADE ME SMILE

TOMORROW'S
INTENTION:

DATE:

So very
Grateful

1.

2.

3.

Today's
Tiny Victory:

That Was Interesting!

tomorrow's intention:

- - - - - - - - - - - - - - - - - -

Date:

So Grateful Today

①

②

③

This was surprising

Today's Tiny Victory:

Tomorrow's Intention:

So grateful for these *PEOPLE!

*super amazing

Date:

This made me smile:

Today's Tiny Victory...

VERY **VERY** GRATEFUL FOR:

1.)

2.)

3.)

Tomorrow's Intention:

DATE:

So Grateful
Today For:
→
→
→

WELL, THIS WAS
interesting!

Today's Tiny Victory:

TOMORROW'S INTENTION:

- -

DATE:

So Grateful
Today For:
①
②
③

Well, This Was Pretty
AWESOME:

Today's Tiny Victory:

TOMORROW'S INTENTION:

Date:

This made me smile:

Today's Tiny Victory...

VERY **VERY** GRATEFUL FOR:

1.)

2.)

3.)

Tomorrow's Intention:

Today's Tiny Victory:

DATE:

THIS WAS PRETTY COOL:

WOW!

I AM SUPER GRATEFUL FOR:

1

2

3

TOMORROW'S INTENTION

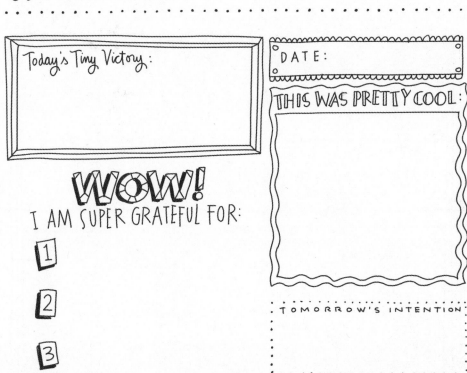

Date:

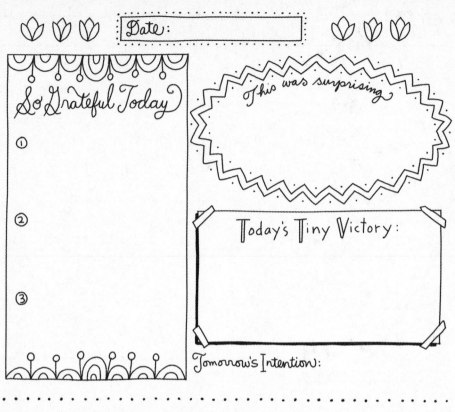

So Grateful Today

①

②

③

This was surprising

Today's Tiny Victory:

Tomorrow's Intention:

my DREAMS

date:

Today I am Grateful for:

① ② ③

+ one more!

Well, this was pretty cool:

TODAY'S TINY VICTORY

TOMORROW'S INTENTION:

SO VERY GRATEFUL FOR:

① ② ③

This made me smile

DATE:

TODAY'S TINY VICTORY

Tomorrow's Intention:

DATE:

So very Grateful

1.

2.

3.

Today's Tiny Victory:

That Was Interesting!

tomorrow's intention:

Date:

Today I Am Grateful For:

1

2

3

TODAY'S tiny VICTORY

OKAY... THIS WAS INTERESTING!

Tomorrow's Intention:

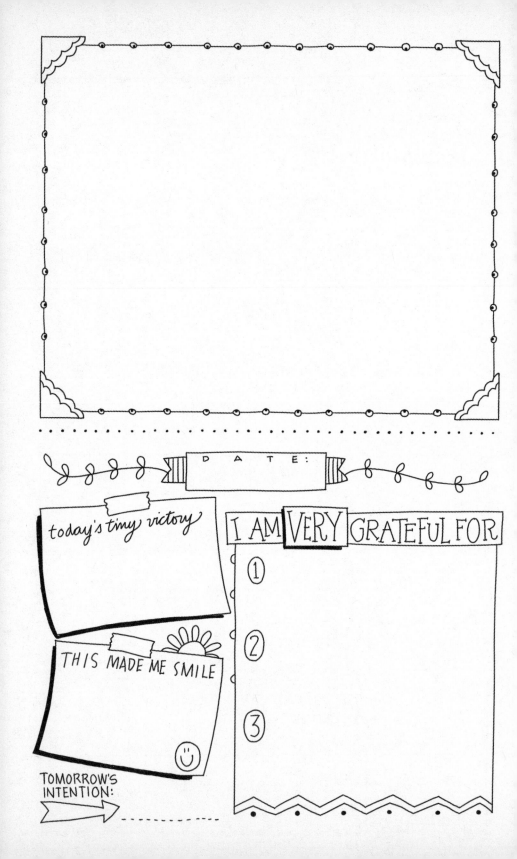

D A T E:

today's tiny victory

I AM VERY GRATEFUL FOR

①

②

③

THIS MADE ME SMILE

TOMORROW'S
INTENTION:

date:

VERY grateful for:

1

2

3

hmmm...this made me think today:

Today's Tiny Victory

TOMORROW'S INTENTION:

I'm So Grateful Today

1.)

2.)

3.)

DATE:

This made me SMILE:

Today's Tiny Victory

Tomorrow's Intention:

Today's Tiny Victory:

DATE:

THIS WAS PRETTY COOL:

WOW!

I AM SUPER GRATEFUL FOR:

1

2

3

TOMORROW'S INTENTION

SO VERY GRATEFUL FOR:

1

2

3

DATE:

TODAY'S TINY VICTORY

This made me smile

❀ Tomorrow's ❀ Intention:

DATE:

So Grateful Today For:

WELL, THIS WAS interesting!

Today's Tiny Victory:

TOMORROW'S INTENTION:

DATE:

So Grateful Today For:

①

②

③

Well, This Was Pretty AWESOME:

Today's Tiny Victory:

TOMORROW'S INTENTION:

Date:

Today I Am Grateful For:

1

2

3

TODAY'S tiny VICTORY

OKAY... THIS WAS INTERESTING!

Tomorrow's Intention:

What If I... ?*

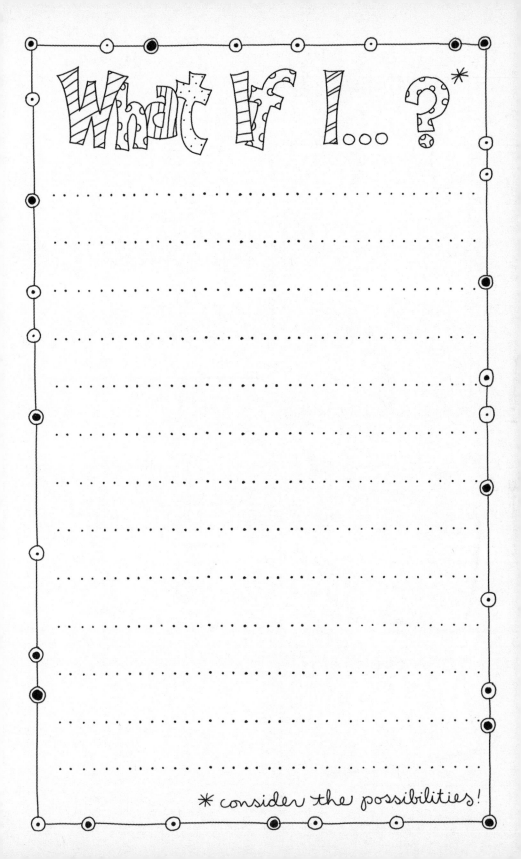

* consider the possibilities!

Date:

So Grateful Today

① ② ③

This was surprising

Today's Tiny Victory:

Tomorrow's Intention:

D A T E:

today's tiny victory

THIS MADE ME SMILE

TOMORROW'S INTENTION:

I AM VERY GRATEFUL FOR

① ② ③

DATE:

So very Grateful

1.

2.

3.

Today's Tiny Victory:

That Was Interesting!

tomorrow's intention:

- -

Today's Tiny Victory:

DATE:

THIS WAS PRETTY COOL:

WOW!
I AM SUPER GRATEFUL FOR:

1

2

3

TOMORROW'S INTENTION

Date:

This made me smile:

Today's Tiny Victory...

VERY **VERY** GRATEFUL FOR:

1.)

2.)

3.)

Tomorrow's Intention:

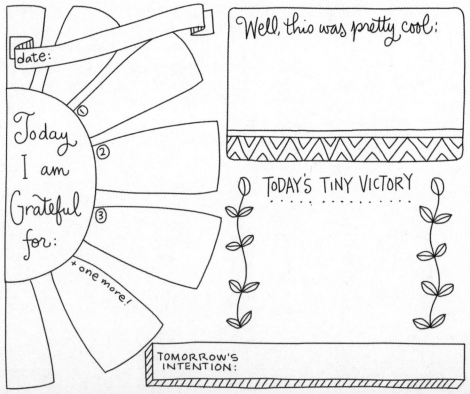

date:

Today I am Grateful for:

① ② ③

+ one more!

Well, this was pretty cool:

TODAY'S TINY VICTORY

TOMORROW'S INTENTION:

SO VERY GRATEFUL FOR...

①

②

③

DATE:

TODAY'S TINY VICTORY

This made me smile

❀ Tomorrow's ❀
Intention:

Date:

So Grateful Today

①

②

③

This was surprising

Today's Tiny Victory:

Tomorrow's Intention:

Lately I've been thinking...

I'm So Grateful Today

1.)

2.)

3.)

DATE:

This made me SMILE:

Today's Tiny Victory

Tomorrow's Intention:

DATE:

So Grateful Today For:

WELL, THIS WAS interesting!

Today's Tiny Victory:

TOMORROW'S INTENTION:

DATE:

So Grateful Today For:

①

②

③

Well, This Was Pretty AWESOME:

Today's Tiny Victory!

TOMORROW'S INTENTION:

date:

VERY grateful for:

①

②

③

hmmm...this made me think today:

Today's Tiny Victory

TOMORROW'S INTENTION:

Today's Tiny Victory:

DATE:

THIS WAS PRETTY COOL:

WOW!

I AM SUPER GRATEFUL FOR:

1

2

3

TOMORROW'S INTENTION

DATE:

So very Grateful

1.

2.

3.

Today's Tiny Victory:

That Was Interesting!

tomorrow's intention:

Date:

This made me smile:

Today's Tiny Victory...

VERY **VERY** GRATEFUL FOR:

1.)

2.)

3.)

Tomorrow's Intention:

Date:

So Grateful Today

①

②

③

This was surprising

Today's Tiny Victory:

Tomorrow's Intention:

ABOUT THE AUTHOR

Ronnie Walter is an artist and award-winning writer. As a professional illustrator, she has licensed her designs onto hundreds of products including stickers, greeting cards, stationery, giftware, home goods, fabric, and more. She is the creative force behind the bestselling Coloring Café® series of adult coloring books and has published both business and fiction books about the artist's life.

Ronnie also teaches and coaches artists and other creatives to help them clarify their goals and move their creative dreams and businesses forward. She lives in a little house by the water with her husband Jim Marcotte and the best shelter dog ever, Larry.

Email: ronnie@ronniewalter.com
Instagram: @ronniewalter
Twitter: @myfriendronnie
www.ronniewalter.com

Mango Publishing, established in 2014, publishes an eclectic list of books by diverse authors—both new and established voices—on topics ranging from business, personal growth, women's empowerment, LGBTQ studies, health, and spirituality to history, popular culture, time management, decluttering, lifestyle, mental wellness, aging, and sustainable living. We were recently named 2019's #1 fastest growing independent publisher by *Publishers Weekly*. Our success is driven by our main goal, which is to publish high quality books that will entertain readers as well as make a positive difference in their lives.

Our readers are our most important resource; we value your input, suggestions, and ideas. We'd love to hear from you—after all, we are publishing books for you!

Please stay in touch with us and follow us at:

Facebook: Mango Publishing
Twitter: @MangoPublishing
Instagram: @MangoPublishing
LinkedIn: Mango Publishing
Pinterest: Mango Publishing

Sign up for our newsletter at www.mango.bz and receive a free book!

Join us on Mango's journey to reinvent publishing, one book at a time.